Best Inventions

Printing Press

by Julie Murray

3

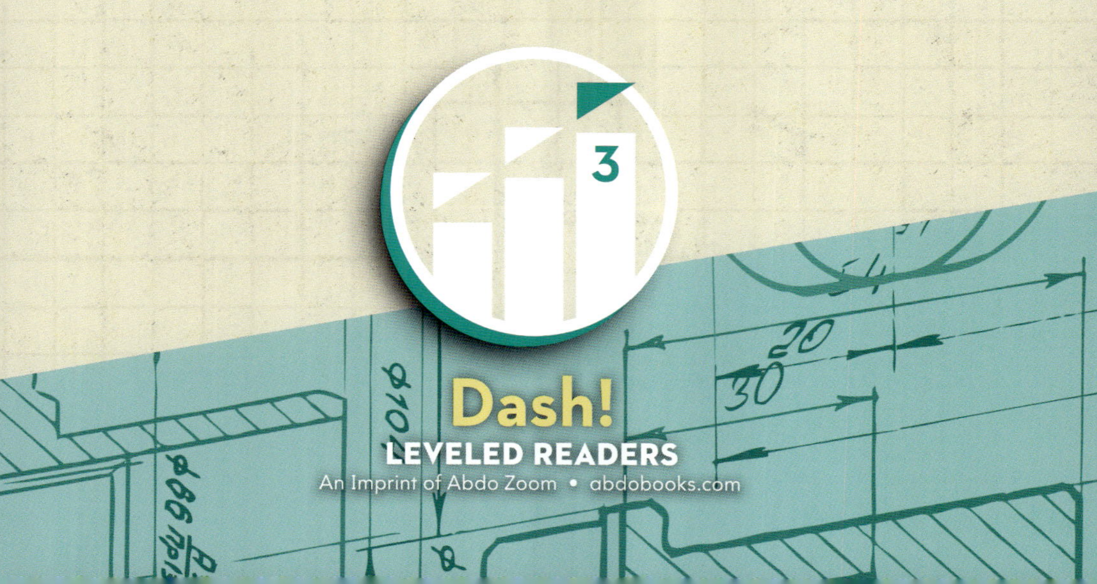

Dash!

LEVELED READERS

An Imprint of Abdo Zoom • abdobooks.com

Level 1 – Beginning
Short and simple sentences with familiar words or patterns for children who are beginning to understand how letters and sounds go together.

Level 2 – Emerging
Longer words and sentences with more complex language patterns for readers who are practicing common words and letter sounds.

Level 3 – Transitional
More developed language and vocabulary for readers who are becoming more independent.

abdobooks.com

Published by Abdo Zoom, a division of ABDO, PO Box 398166, Minneapolis, Minnesota 55439.
Copyright © 2023 by Abdo Consulting Group, Inc. International copyrights reserved in all countries.
No part of this book may be reproduced in any form without written permission from the publisher.
Dash!™ is a trademark and logo of Abdo Zoom.

Printed in the United States of America, North Mankato, Minnesota.
102022
012023

Photo Credits: Alamy, Getty Images, Shutterstock
Production Contributors: Kenny Abdo, Jennie Forsberg, Grace Hansen, John Hansen
Design Contributors: Candice Keimig, Neil Klinepier, Colleen McLaren

Library of Congress Control Number: 2022937313

Publisher's Cataloging in Publication Data

Names: Murray, Julie, author.
Title: Printing Press / by Julie Murray
Description: Minneapolis, Minnesota : Abdo Zoom, 2023 | Series: Best inventions | Includes online
    resources and index.
Identifiers: ISBN 9781098280185 (lib. bdg.) | ISBN 9781098280710 (ebook) | ISBN 9781098281014
    (Read-to-Me ebook)
Subjects: LCSH: Printing presses--Juvenile literature. | Inventions--Juvenile literature. | Printing--History--
    Juvenile literature. | Inventions--History--Juvenile literature.
Classification: DDC 769.9--dc23

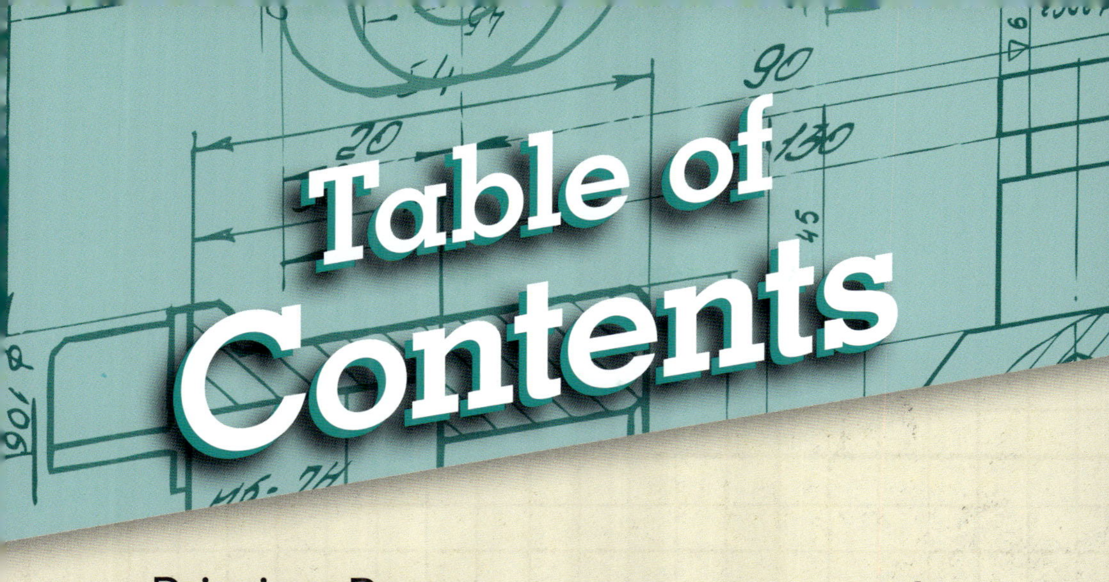

Table of Contents

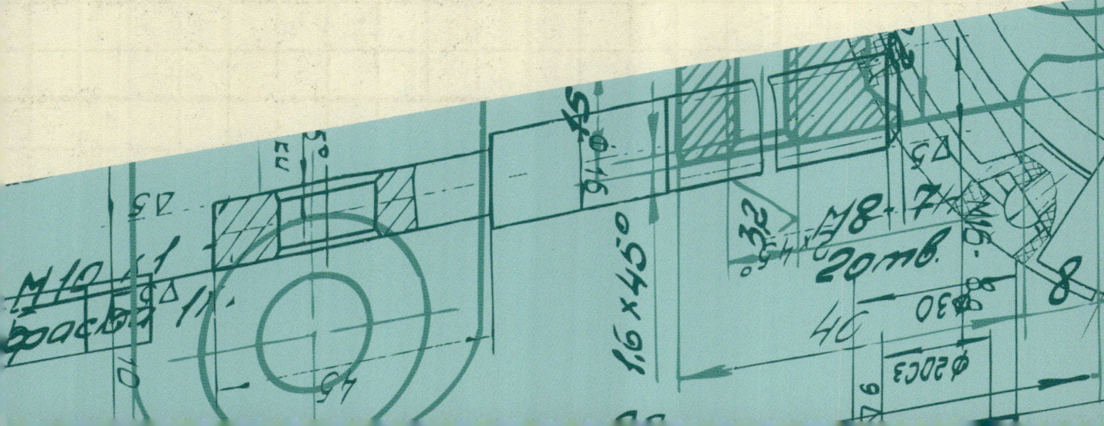

Printing Press

The printing press is a machine that creates copies of written text or images. It is an invention that changed the world!

History

Woodblock printing was first used in China long ago. **Characters** were carved into a woodblock. Ink was applied to them. Silk or cloth was then pressed onto the block. This process was perfected using paper by the end of the 9th century.

軍政府
願
可憐
可憐
諸君
速速
來救
諸位
得其
善惡
一則
二無

In the 11th century, Chinese inventor Bi Sheng created moveable type printing. Each **ceramic** piece had a **character** carved into it. The pieces could be moved around and reused.

Johannes Gutenberg, a German **goldsmith** born around 1400, improved the process. He used metal to make individual letters and symbols. He also created a new type of oil-based ink.

יברכך יהוה, וישמרך
פניו אליך ויחנך
פניו אליך
o Sen
a resp
sto sob
ericord
o Sen
ante
sto, e

Around 1440, Gutenberg created the first printing press. It was a device that transferred ink from moveable type to paper. It did this by using pressure to press the type to the paper.

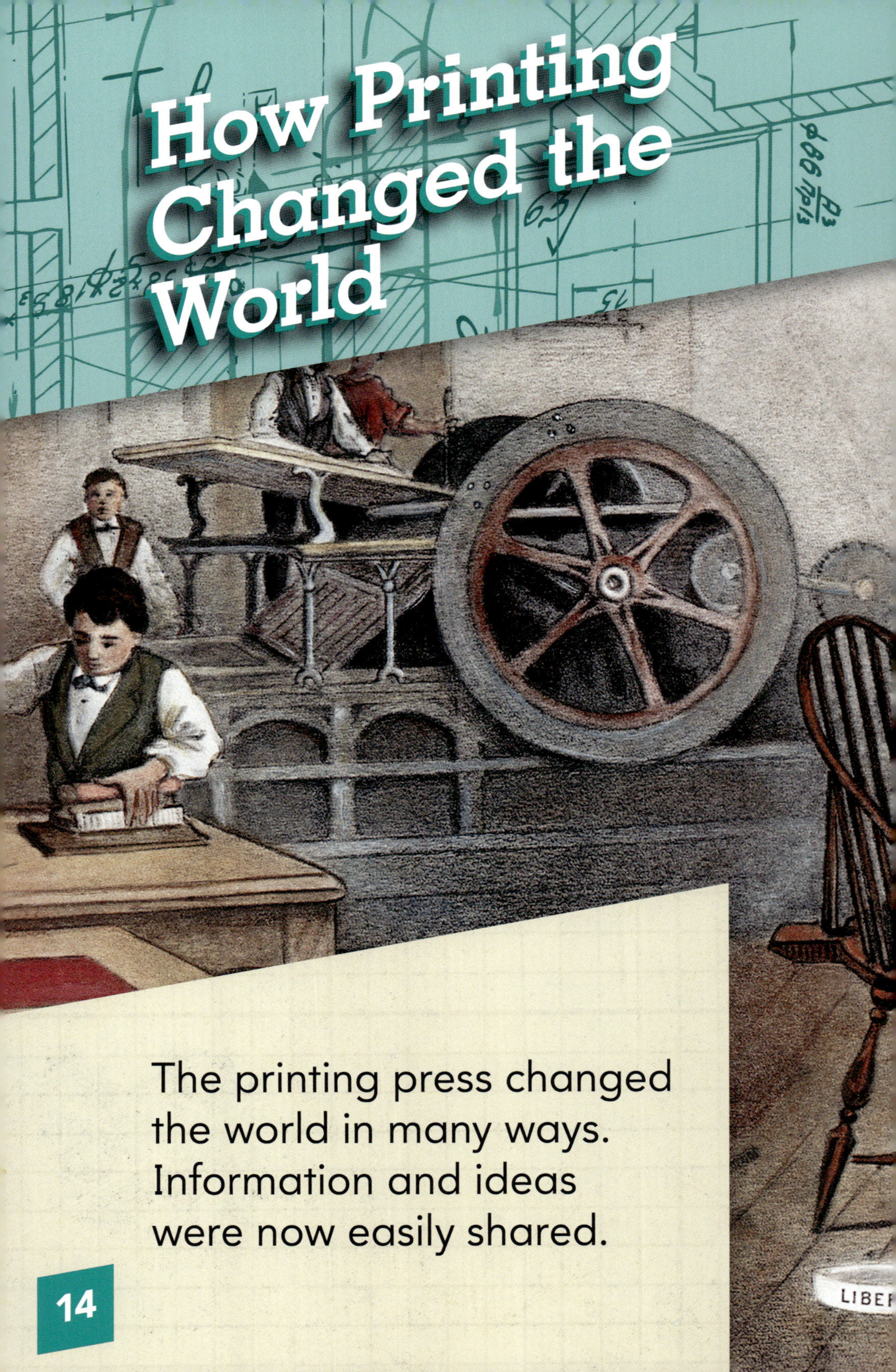

How Printing Changed the World

The printing press changed the world in many ways. Information and ideas were now easily shared.

GLORY TO GOD IN THE HIGHEST. ON EARTH PEACE. GOOD WILL TOWARD MEN.
ND UNION NOW AND FOR EVER
ONE AND INSEPARABLE
15

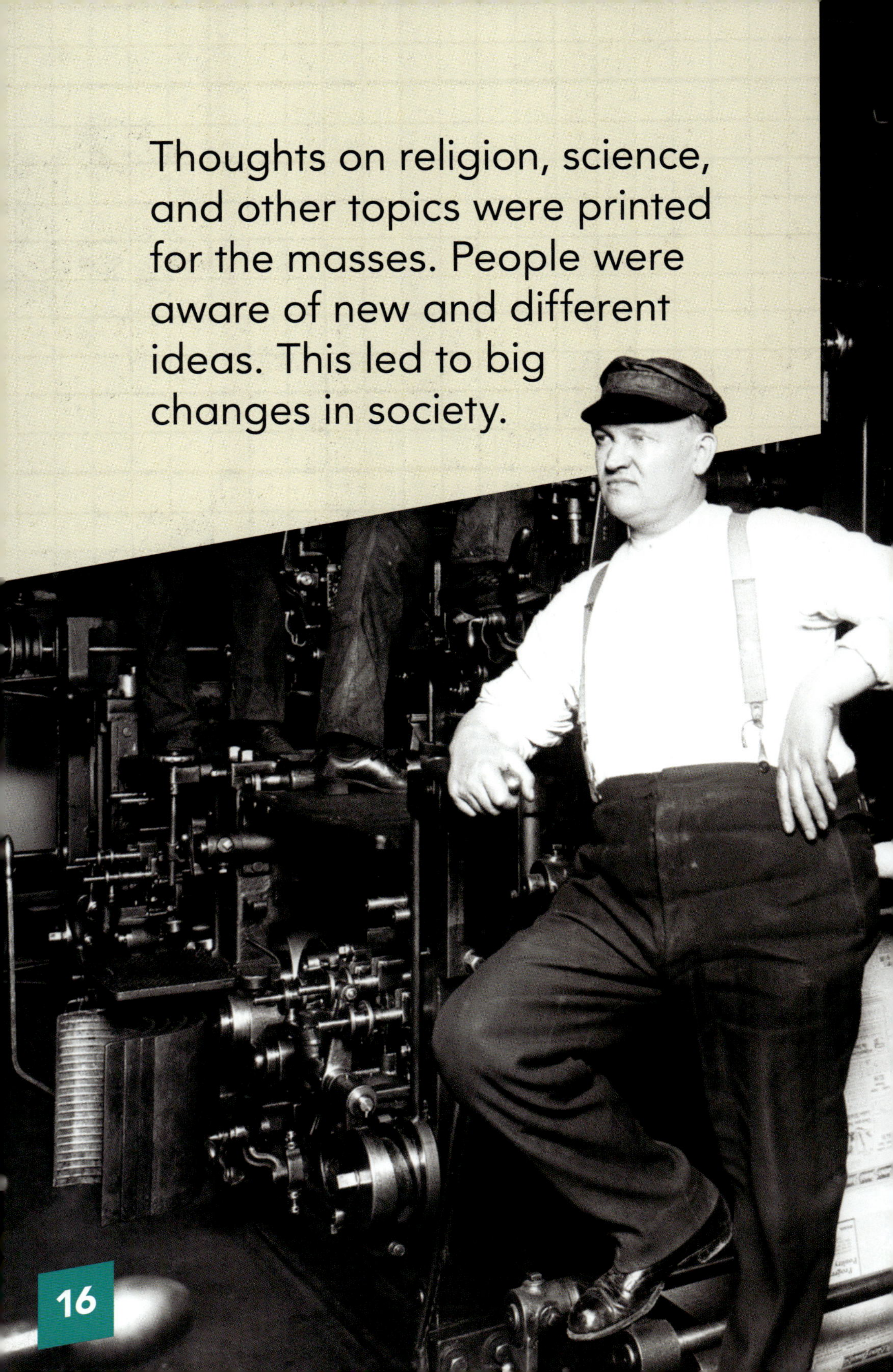

Thoughts on religion, science, and other topics were printed for the masses. People were aware of new and different ideas. This led to big changes in society.

THE GOSS PRINTING PRESS
CHICAGO ILL U S A
THE GOSS PRINTING
PATENTED
STRAIGHT LINE REPERF
CHICAGO
THE PUEBLO CHIEFTAIN
Elegant Furniture 10 20 30 40 50

The printing press also helped more people learn how to read. People had a **desire** to gain knowledge from newspapers, fliers, and books.

Printing presses are still being used today. They have been **modernized** over the years. **Digital printing** is also a popular and easy way to print.

- The *Diamond Sutra* is the oldest-known printed book. It was published in China around 868 CE.

- The Gutenberg Bible, also called the 42-line Bible, was the first book printed in Europe using moveable type. It was printed around 1455.

- Nearly 130 million different books have been printed in the world.

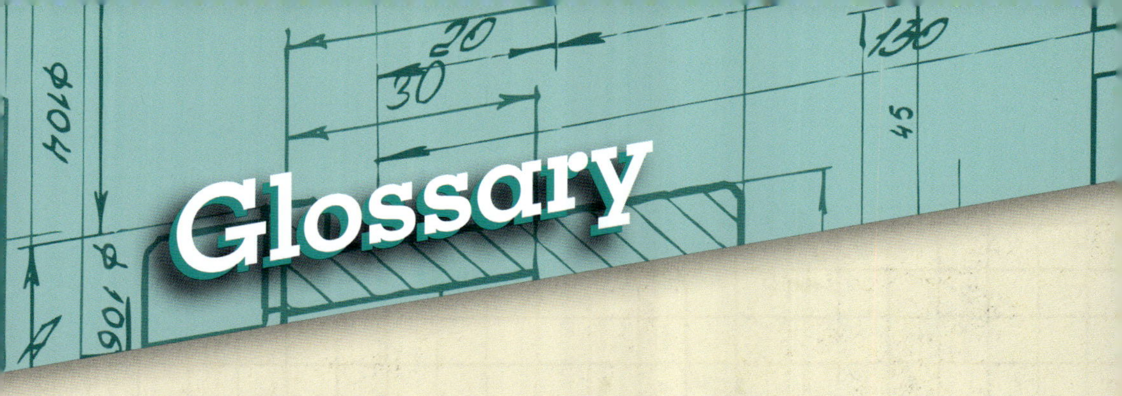

Glossary

ceramic – of or having to do with objects made of baked clay.

characters – in Chinese writing, symbols or signs used to represent the Chinese language.

desire – to want or wish for.

digital printing – a method of printing that makes prints from electronic files.

goldsmith – one who makes or sells objects of gold.

modernized – brought up to date or improved with new technology.

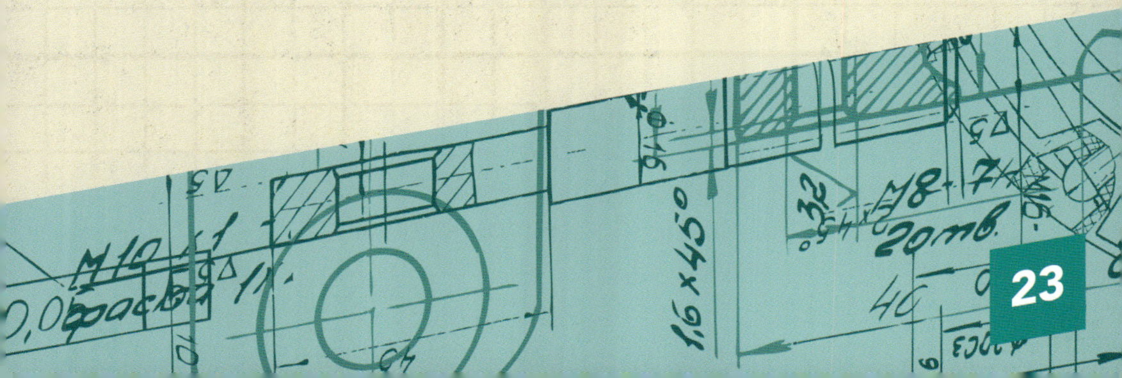

Index

Online Resources

Booklinks
NONFICTION NETWORK
FREE! ONLINE NONFICTION RESOURCES

To learn more about printing presses, please visit **abdobooklinks.com** or scan this QR code. These links are routinely monitored and updated to provide the most current information available.